It is Sunday morning. Karen o[ ]
house.

'Hello!' she says. 'Are you the
Karen's father writes books.
about art. He opens the door of his study.

'Ah, Karen,' he says. 'You're home.'

'Yes, Dad,' Karen says. 'And I'm tired. I was in Geneva yesterday and in Paris on Friday.'

'Were you?' her father says. He looks surprised.

'Dad, it's my job. You know that.'

'Oh, yes,' her father says. 'Now come into my study. I want to show you some pictures.'

In the study there are books on the table, on the chairs and on the floor.

'Dad!' Karen says. 'Look at this room!'

'Why? What's wrong with it?'

'Books, books, books!' Karen says. 'Can I clean it for you?'

'No!' her father says. 'I like it. Now, Karen, look at these beautiful pictures.'

'They're wonderful,' Karen says. 'Are you going to put them in your new book?'

'Yes, but I can only put one in the book,' her father says.

'I like this picture,' says Karen.

'Good girl,' her father says. 'You understand art, Karen. I like that picture too.'

'Thanks, Dad. Now, what do you want to eat?'

On Monday, Karen gets up early. She takes a taxi to the airport. She is going to work again.

She stands at the door of the aeroplane and smiles at the passengers.

'Hello! Good morning,' she says.

People come into the aeroplane and sit down. Karen brings them drinks and food.

The aeroplane flies to Rome, and Karen says goodbye to the passengers. She has no work in the afternoon. She is flying from Rome tomorrow morning.

She goes to her hotel room. She washes and she drinks some coffee. Then she goes into the street.

Karen loves Rome. She loves the old buildings, the shops and the cafés. She walks for a long time.

It is hot, and Karen is tired. She sees a little café. She walks across the street and goes in.

'Yes?' the barman asks.

'A Fanta, please,' Karen says.

There are a lot of pictures in the café. Karen looks at them. They are all beautiful.

'These pictures are wonderful!' Karen says to the barman. 'Who's the artist?'

The barman looks unhappy.

'Don't talk to me about that artist,' he says. 'He comes here every day. He eats my food, but he never gives me any money. He gives me these pictures.'

'But they're wonderful!' Karen says. 'He's a good artist. What's his name?'

'You can ask him,' the barman says. 'Look, he's coming in now.'

The artist is a young man with dark brown hair. He is thin and he looks tired.

'Please,' he says to the barman, 'give me some food and a drink.'

'No!' the barman says. 'Every day you come in here. Every day you ask for food. But you never pay me! Where's your money? Give me some money, and then you can eat.'

The artist is angry. 'But I always pay you,' he says. 'I give you my pictures. Today I've got a new picture for you. Look at it!'

'Now listen to me, Antonio Brunetti,' the barman says. 'I don't want pictures. I want money. You haven't got any? Go away.'

Karen stands up. 'Oh please,' she says, 'can I see the picture?'

Antonio looks at Karen. 'Who are you?' he asks.

'I'm a visitor in Rome,' Karen says. 'I love your pictures. They're wonderful.'

'Are they?' Antonio says.

Karen smiles. 'Yes, they are. Can I buy your new picture, please?'

'Don't buy a picture from *him*,' the barman says. 'I've got a lot of his pictures. You can buy *them*.'

Antonio is looking at Karen. 'You're a beautiful woman,' he says, 'and you like my art. Take my picture. It's yours.'

'Oh, I can't,' Karen says. 'It's a good picture. You can sell it for a lot of money.'

Antonio smiles, but he isn't happy.

'Sell it?' he says. 'How? People don't buy my pictures. They don't like them. Only you.'

Karen thinks about this. 'All right,' she says. 'Give me your picture, Antonio. I can take it with me to London tomorrow.'

'You're going to London tomorrow?' Antonio says. He is unhappy. 'But I want to paint a picture of you.'

'Oh!' says Karen. Then she smiles. 'I'm coming to Rome again in a week.'

'I can paint you then,' Antonio says.

'All right,' Karen says. 'But now I'm going to buy some pictures.' She looks at the pictures on the café wall. 'I want this picture...' she says slowly, 'and I want that picture too...'

She gives the barman some money. 'This is for the pictures,' she says, 'and for food. We want to eat now, please.'

A day later, Karen is at home again.

'Dad!' she says. 'Look at these pictures. What do you think?'

Her father looks at Antonio's pictures. He looks for a long time.

'They're very, very good,' he says. 'Wonderful. Where are they from?'

'From Rome,' Karen says. 'I want to sell them. The artist needs money.'

Karen's father shakes his head. 'The pictures are very good,' he says, 'but people don't know this artist. How are you going to sell them? It's going to be difficult.'

'I know,' Karen says. 'But I'm going to do it, Dad. Antonio's a good artist.'

Karen takes a picture and telephones for a taxi. She takes the taxi to Bond Street and goes into an art gallery. The gallery is small but expensive. A woman is sitting at a table. She is reading a book.

'Hello,' she says.

'Good afternoon,' Karen says. 'I've got a picture here, and I want to sell it.'

'Who's the artist?' The woman doesn't look up.

'Antonio Brunetti,' Karen says. 'He's . . .'

'I'm sorry.' The woman starts to read her book again. 'I don't know that name.'

A man comes into the gallery. 'I've got a new Sherman for you!' he says. 'It's wonderful.'

'Who?' the woman says.

'Oh, you know him,' the man says. 'Sherman! He's got an exhibition at the Galerie Saint Michel in Paris!'

'Oh!' The woman puts down her book. 'Let's see. Yes, I like it. Sherman, you said? I can give you £800.'

Quietly, Karen goes away.

She walks across the street and goes into the Astra Gallery.

'I've got a wonderful new Brunetti for you,' she says to the man. 'Look at this.'

'What?' the man says. 'Who's Brunetti?'

'Oh, you know him,' Karen says. 'He's got an exhibition at the Leonardo in Rome.'

'Oh,' the man says. 'Show me.' He looks at the picture. 'Very good,' he says. 'Brunetti, eh? At the Leonardo? OK. I can give you . . . £900.'

Karen is very happy, but she doesn't smile.

'Hmm . . .' she says.

'All right, £1,000,' the man says.

'OK,' Karen says.

The man gives her a cheque for £1,000.

'Thank you,' Karen says.

In the afternoon, Karen is working again. This time, she flies to Paris. Later, she takes a taxi to a place with a lot of art galleries. She looks at them, and then she goes into a small, expensive gallery.

'Hello,' she says. 'I've got a wonderful picture for you. A new Brunetti! Look!'

'Who's Brunetti?' the man says.

'Brunetti?' Karen says. 'He's going to be famous. He's got a big exhibition at the Leonardo in Rome, and a small exhibition at the Astra Gallery in London.'

The man likes the picture, and he gives Karen a cheque for a lot of money.

Karen is very happy. She takes a taxi to the airport. In the evening, she flies to Amsterdam.

A week later, Karen is in Rome again. She goes to the Café Leonardo.

'Where's Antonio?' she says to the barman.

'I don't know,' the barman says. 'He doesn't come here now.'

Karen is unhappy. She walks to the door. A young man is sitting at a table. He stands up and talks to her.

'Excuse me,' he says. 'Are you Karen from England? You liked Antonio's pictures. He often talks about you. I'm his friend – my name's Giorgio.'

'Where is he?' Karen asks. 'Where's Antonio?'

'He's in bed,' Giorgio says. 'He's ill today. He's not very strong. He's got no money, and he doesn't eat well.'

'Can you take me to him?' Karen asks. 'I want to see him.'

Karen walks with Giorgio. She walks quickly because she wants to see Antonio. Then she sees a food shop.

'Please, Giorgio,' she says. 'Can you wait for me?'

She goes into the shop and buys a lot of food and drink.

Giorgio stops at an old house. 'Antonio's in here,' he says.

Karen goes in behind him, and Giorgio opens a door.

'Antonio! Look! Karen's here!' he says. Antonio is ill, and he can't stand up. But he smiles at Karen.

'It's you!' he says. 'You're here! This is wonderful.'

'Hello, Antonio,' Karen says quietly.

'Don't go away again,' Antonio says. 'I . . . I want to paint you.'

'You can't paint me today,' Karen says. 'You're not well.'

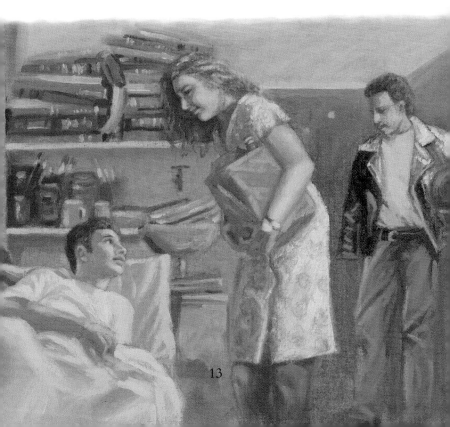

'I'm OK,' Antonio says.

'You don't look OK,' Karen says. 'You need good food and a clean room.'

'But I haven't got any money,' Antonio says. 'People don't buy my pictures.'

'Yes, they do,' Karen says. 'Look!'

She takes a lot of money from her bag.

'What's this?' Antonio says.

'This money's for your pictures. Your work's now in very good galleries in London, Paris and Amsterdam!'

'What? My pictures?' Antonio is very surprised.

Karen starts to put the money into Antonio's hands. But he doesn't want it. He wants to take Karen's hands. The money falls to the floor.

'Don't give money to Antonio,' Giorgio smiles. 'He doesn't understand money.'

Karen smiles too.

'He needs you,' Giorgio says. 'Listen. You can work with Antonio. He can paint the pictures, and you can sell them for him.'

'Yes!' Antonio says.

'OK,' Karen says. 'Why not? And now, Antonio, I'm going to make some food!'

Antonio and Giorgio eat and eat.

Later, Antonio says, 'That was wonderful. Don't go away again, Karen. I want to paint you. In a red dress! A blue dress! In this room! In a garden . . .'

'But I'm flying to London this afternoon,' Karen says. 'I'm going to sell your pictures, remember? But I'm going to come here again.'

'And one day,' Antonio says, 'you're going to stay here.'

Karen smiles. 'Who knows?'

ACTIVITIES

Before you read

1 Look at the pictures on pages 1–7. Talk about the people in the pictures. Who are they? What do they do?

2 Look at the Word List at the back of the book. Then make sentences with these words.
   a pay, cheque
   b artist, gallery
   c passenger, fly
   d need, tired
   e clean, study

While you read

3 Are these sentences right (✓) or wrong (✗)?
   a Karen's father writes about art.   .....
   b Karen works on trains.   .....
   c She doesn't like Rome.   .....
   d The barman wants money, not pictures.   .....
   e Antonio hasn't got any money.   .....
   f Karen buys some pictures from Antonio.   .....

After you read

4 Who is talking? What are they talking about?
   a 'Dad, it's my job.'
   b 'Good girl.'
   c 'He comes here every day.'
   d 'It's yours.'

5 What is Karen going to do with the pictures? Why? What do you think?

Before you read

6 Work with a friend. Karen is in England again.

  Student A: You are Karen's father. Ask questions about the pictures.

  Student B: You are Karen. Answer your father's questions.

While you read

7 Finish these sentences. Write one word in every sentence.

 a Karen's father likes Antonio's ....

 b Karen wants to .... them for Antonio.

 c But galleries only want the work of .... artists.

 d Karen talks about .... of Antonio's work in important galleries.

 e Then people .... a lot of money for the pictures.

 f Antonio isn't strong because he doesn't eat ....

 g Karen gives Antonio ...., but he doesn't take it.

 h Antonio is going to .... pictures and Karen is going to sell them for him.

After you read

8 You are Karen. Write to Antonio in London. What are you doing? When are you going to see him again?

9 You are Antonio. Write to Karen from Rome. You want to see her every day. You want to paint her.

WORD LIST *with example sentences*

art (n) I like looking at *art*, but I don't want to talk to the *artists*.

cheque (n) My money is at home, but I can write a *cheque*.

clean (adj/v) We aren't going to stay in this hotel again. The rooms aren't *clean*.

Dad (n) I go to football games with my *Dad*.

exhibition (n) We are going to see an *exhibition* of Van Gogh's pictures.

fly (v) I can take the train to London and then *fly* to Paris.

gallery (n) You can buy his pictures from a *gallery* in Manchester.

need (v) I do two jobs because I *need* the money.

paint (v) He is *painting* a picture of my sister.

passenger (n) There are only thirty or forty *passengers* on this aeroplane.

pay (v) Can I *pay* you tomorrow? I haven't got any money with me.

pound (n) The black dress is thirty *pounds*, and the blue dress is twenty.

sell (v) He is *selling* his old car. He wants a new car.

shake (v) I ask for money, but he *shakes* his head.

show (v) *Show* me your homework. Is it difficult?

study (n) At home, she works in her *study*.

surprised (adj) He is a doctor now. I am *surprised* because he wasn't a very good student at school.

tired (adj) I am very *tired*. I didn't sleep well.

wall (n) She is going to put the new picture on her kitchen *wall*.

wonderful (adj) We had a *wonderful* holiday in Italy. We loved it.

Pearson Education Limited
Edinburgh Gate, Harlow,
Essex CM20 2JE, England
and Associated Companies throughout the world.

ISBN: 978-1-4058-7667-4

First published 2000
This edition first published 2008

1 3 5 7 9 10 8 6 4 2

Copyright © Pearson Education Ltd 2008
Illustrations by Stephen Jones

Typeset by Graphicraft Ltd, Hong Kong
Set in 12/14pt Bembo
Printed in China
SWTC/01

Published by Pearson Education Ltd in association with
Penguin Books Ltd, both companies being subsidiaries of Pearson Plc